SHELTER IN PLACE

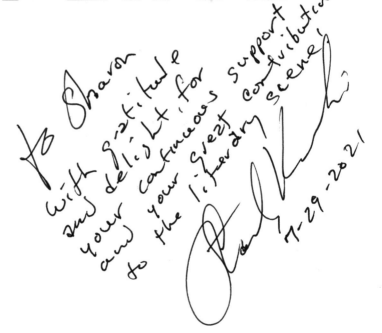

To Sharon
with gratitude
and delight for
your continuous support
and your great contribution
to the literary scene.

7-29-2021

SHELTER IN PLACE

Pandemic Poems

Stanley Kusunoki

Polaris
Publicattions

An impirint of
North Star Press of St. Cloud Inc.
www.northstarpress.com

Cover art and design by Jay Monroe

Polaris Publications
 an imprint of North Star Press of St. Cloud Inc.
w w w . n o r t h s t a r p r e s s . c o m

ISBN: 978-1-68201-123-2

First Edition

Contents

Foreword

When the governor of Minnesota announced that schools would be closed because of the COVID-19 virus, I sensed this was a historical time unlike any other. Feeling that it was likely to last a while, I started to document my life as a teacher and citizen living under the "Shelter in Place" order.

As days grew into weeks it became evident that stay at home was going to be the new normal—long enough that I would have material for a new manuscript. Here it is.

The poems in this book cover the span from when the Shelter in Place order was announced, to the day that the order was semi-rescinded. The challenges of teaching online, to the day-to-day doing things in a new way, are all here.

Just as we were nearing the end of the school year, another traumatic event shook our lives—the killing of George Floyd by a Minneapolis cop. The shock and reverberations that resulted put more questioning and stress to the end of an already traumatic school year. My response to that will be in a forthcoming collection, since that is outside of the time frame for this book.

The combination of COVID-19 and George Floyd's murder have had massive worldwide impact. Combined with global warming, there is a clear message: *Things must change, and the change must start immediately.*

Let us, as adults, kick-start this change and support the children I teach, their peers, and the young adults I have taught over the last fifteen years— that they may realize a world of promise, justice, and peace.

Stanley Kusunoki
June 2020

Again and Again

Just when we get cocky
Think we rule the world
Smug in our superiority
The smallest thing
Single cell
Can't even see it
Wreaks havoc upon us all

Call it Black Plague
Smallpox
AIDS
Avian Flu
Swine Flu
MERS
SARS
Ebola
Now, COVID-19
All cause us great beings
To panic, hoard
Rat brain
Stock up stock up stock up
Us not them

And yet
They call out
"Where is the best
Of your humanity?"

A gauntlet thrown down
For us to pick up
By getting past fear
To the big picture

The test

Shutdown

The school is not happy
Only teachers'
footsteps today
not the thundering
Packs of fifth graders
Chattering third graders
Skip-dancing kindergarteners
No
Everything muted at a muted pace
Teachers
In hushed groups
(six feet away from
each other please)

Everywhere it is wait and see
in the place where
it is usually
always movement
always chatter
always something

The school sulks
yearns for a quick death
to micro-organisms
and a quick return
of its heartbeat

Shutdown, Part 2

It feels like the end of school
Just a trickle of kids out to the busses
Three black cars up top for pick up
From the upper lot we look down
Buslines done, back inside
Heads down, slow shoe shuffle

Back in the building
The safety net
Forms
Promises of chat sites
Connections continuing
The elastic bond
Of this group of teachers
Knitting together
A web of care and support

Shutdown Part 3

This is
UNschool
Time disjointed
Marked by clicking
"next" to move
Yet another training session
Break
Walk around the block
More training

Now it is the interruptions
That are the relief
Google meet with a teacher pal
Emails from parents
A photo bomb
From a fifth grader
Connections

The Weekend

Saturday morning
The Christmas cactus
Stretches its arms up
To sunlight through
The bay window

Cars up Lexington Ave.
A whispering whoosh
Better for the writer
Searching for words

The weekend
Yes, but not really
The days flow together
In semi-confinement
No families piling out
Of their Subarus
And Ford Escapes
For a day at the zoo

No kite flyers in the park
Nor games at the athletic fields
"Weekend Edition"
On the radio
The only clue

Vernal Equinox 2020

"You must believe in spring…"
Goes the song
And so must we all
In this time of isolation
Life still turns in its cycles
Green speartips
Break the crust of dirt
and snow scrum
Ground squirrels scurry
from their burrows
Magnolia buds begin
puffing out
A flurry of action at the birdfeeder
we search the yard
for the first sighting
of Boss Robin

Nature's therapy
for us—
Take a break
Get off the computer
The news
social media
step outside
Breathe
look deeply and watch
The resilient world
Returning to life

Online Meeting

It was a disaster
First Zoom meeting
With the students
Chatty kids tripping over each other
The software trying to keep up
The prominent voices hogging
The screen

But orderly discourse
Not the point
This time at least
Craving the joy
The energy
Of the students
Shut-ins interacting
Reason enough

The learning for next time:
Mute the mics

Isolation

What better way to isolate
Than in a car?
Glass and metal
(in my case, Saturn's polycarbonate)
Keep others away
Even isolated from pavement
By rolling rubber

A sunny day escape
CD in the player
The healing
Of trees
And sky
And two-lane blacktop

Exception made
Chocolate shop in Marine
(a necessity!)
Then across the St. Croix
And a stop
Oh, flowing water!

Trees
Sky
Water
Music
Chocolates
And an open road
Good medicine

Prayers With the Ancestors

Oh Gramps, Oh Grams
I am glad you are safe
From contagion
From worries:
Who's sick?
Who's dead?
You still giving us
Wisdom
Patience
Calm

The same too
Mom and dad
Pearl, you know
You would be up all night
Worrying about your sister, brother
Family in Hong Kong
And Tokyo
All the cousins
You writing missives
In your precise cursive

And dad
Shut out from friends
Dinners at Sakura
And Salut
Missing jazzy moments
At Crooners
Even the Como Pavillion
That would not do

So we are here
In the space we left
Your material being
Understanding the spirits
Travel with us
We are OK
We are carrying on
What you started
Stay with us
Strengthen us
Grant us your fortitude
Grant us peace

The New Classroom

The new classroom
Looks a lot like my dining room table
Instead of place settings
Notebooks, papers, class rosters
Assorted lesson books
And the ubiquitous MacBook

The new classroom
Is a 13-inch screen
No SmartBoard
No jumble of desks and chairs
No postings of student work
(although yes, there are a couple of
Homework sheets flopped on the table
Napping, it seems)

The new classroom
Just the grey noise
Of radio
The latest in the outbreak
Official announcements
And more blah blah

The new classroom
Is no substitute
For the real thing
For real contact
The glee of greeting
The moans of complaints
The scratch of pencil
To paper
The triumph
Of lightbulbs switching
On and on and on
Like a galaxy of neurons
Firing in synch

Shelter In Place

"Gimme Shelter"
"Shelter from the Storm"
How many times does "Shelter"
Pop up in our lexicon of lyrics?
And now today
Not a pop-melody
But a Governor's order
Shelter
Batten down the hatches
Bolt the door
Close the gates
Shut down
Shut in
But don't shut up
Don't close out friends
Neighbors
Community

Listen!
In the streets
And balconies of Italy
The Gonda Building
At Mayo Clnic
People singing out
In all genres
In all languages
A massed anthem
Of voices
Raised

More sturdy than
Wooden gates
Metal bolts
Walls of stone
Here is shelter
That will keep us whole
That will keep us sane
That will keep us in touch
Yeah, Mick
Yeah, Bobby
Give us shelter
The carapace of music

11

Walks

Our vacation
A daily walk around the block
Down to the lake
Not much by athletic standards
But enough for us

The chatter of birds
Cardinals
Chickadee
Sparrows
Finch
A lone grackle
The checkmark of geese
Flying to the lake up-north

A child on a scooter
His own lone
Race course down the old
Walk bridge in Como Park

Wary but friendly smile
From a jogger
A Woman from the other
Side of the block
Man with an Irish setter

The soft squish of our shoes
The puddles reflecting
March grey
All just enough
To take a break
Our tiny vacation in place

(un)Intended Consequences

The president says
"the Chinese virus"
As if the Chinese invented it
Cooked it up in
Clandestine laboratories
To spread disease and death
To the world
Like the Europeans dreamed up
The Black Death
To control population
Or they invented
Smallpox
To decimate the Indigenous
American peoples
And of course, didn't Africans
Create Ebola
And AIDS
So we would have an excuse
To ostracize and isolate

The president says
"the Chinese virus"
But it's not racist
No, no
Leave that to his rabid
Bootlickers
Afraid of anyone
Non-Caucasian
An excuse to vent
Signs on stoops
Comments in grocery lines
Contemptuous glances
From a safe distance

The president says
"The Chinese Virus"
In a time of pulling together
He still finds ways to divide

Instead of discourse
Epithets
Instead of understanding
Fear
Instead of intellect
Rat brain
Instead of empathy
Narcissism

So much for government
Of the people
By the people
For the people

Concert in Dangerous Times

New York
America's viral epicenter
And...Heeeere's....Deni
In her seventh floor flat
Singing and playing her heart out
With breaks for toasts
Shout-outs
Taking requests
As live a concert
We are likely to get

She's got her schtick
She's got her lion's head violin
And her blue violin
And as many moves
As she can do
While sitting down in front
Of a videocam

So, for nearly ninety minutes
In her domain
Far from dire news reports
And asshole tweets
(did she time it for the
Daily press self-aggrandizement?)

Ninety minutes
Of smiling
In an unsmiling evening
Ninety minutes
Of tapping toes
Of jiving in place

Ninety minutes
An inoculation
Against worry and fear
Against malaise
Against the closing times
Play on dear Deni
Play on!

15

Grocery Shopping

Heading down to Cub
Takes major planning
Double check the list
Can we get something here
instead of another trip
to TJ's or the corner store
or the co-op?
Make sure the hand wipes
are in the car
Plan a route for
maximum efficiency
and minimum encounters

Six feet
six feet
six feet please
the size of a grave
Waiting for folks
to clear the space
in front of canned tuna
and crushed tomatoes

The shopping goddess
blesses us
The butcher just opening
a new shipment of catfish
The aisle stocker
Hands full, a new case
of toilet paper
Such are the joys
of shopping
These days

Second Weekend

Another weekend
Of a week that wasn't

Oh sure,
We worked on lessons
Did virtual meetings
Called family, friends
Too much time on Facebook

Not time as we know it
Few routines

Days differentiated
By the growing sunlight
Writing a card to far-flung friends
What CD I decide
To pop in the boombox
What tune to play
On the guitar

The Shrinking Circle

A month ago, it was China
Three weeks ago
Washington state
Italy
Spain
New Orleans
New York
Minnesota

Last week it was
The brother of our Lieutenant Governor
Our Senator's husband
Yesterday
It was a writer pal
No one will go untouched

No matter how well
We bar the door
Shelter in place
Wash our hands

We cannot sanitize it
Out of our lives
What is already here

Sunday Paper

Doesn't have as much heft
Not many inserts
Businesses closed or
Take out only restaurants

The Sports section
Articles about what could have been
Trades and maneuvering
Seasons delayed
Seasons deleted

And Entertainment
Online book reviews
But no concerts
Movie reviews
Events on hold

What's left
Mostly Coronavirus
Its ripples
Acts of kindness
A governor's wisdom
A president's callousness
The politics of stupidity

And the comics
Thank God
For the "funny papers"

Church

Yes, it is a video
On a thirteen-inch
Laptop screen
But still
It is a comfort

Even before the service begins
Camera focused on the altar
Wood-paneled wall
The cross
Draped in purple

A place outside our
Shuttered doors and windows
Familiar
We settle in at the kitchen bar
In expectation

We are not disappointed
Music and scripture
Tech malfunctions
Wisdom and prayer
A holy theater

The choir
One member from each section
Sings,
It is our Greek chorus
Responding to Sarah's prayers
Laughing along with Eli'Jah
As his phone app refuses
To respond to the call for offering
Giggles and "Amens"
At appropriate pauses
In Christian's sermon

And after the benediction
The choir leads us out
A recessional.
"He's got the Whole World
In his Hands…"
Back to our kitchen
Just as we were
Before church
But inside
The spirit recharged
And hopeful
Full of Grace

Prayers of Intercession

God have mercy
On all of those infected
With COVID-19
And especially ones closer
To our homes and hearts

Andy
Whose call for poetic resistance
To racism, mindlessness
Vanished ethics
Mobilized pens
Word processors
Even Smith-Coronas
With sticking consonant keys
To stand firm against injustice

And Nachito
Whose hands
On the piano
Transports us all
To his native Cuba
Piano keys melody
And percussion
Driving the passion
From fingers to our limbs
Hips, legs, arms akimbo

God grant that
Energy
Heart
Wisdom
Come full circle
Filling our souls
Our bodies
As we resist
Resist
Resist
The contagion
And return to us
Stronger of heart and mind

Virtual Happy Hour

We are not unique in this
In fact, late to the party
The desire to connect
In these times results
In video
From living room
To back porch
To basement den
Chips and dips
Crackers and cheese
And hoisting a glass
To the computer screen

Al and I however
Are neophytes here
Analog guys in the digital age
It takes several attempts
And switching apps
To see the moving
Image of each other
On the screen

Judy goes to make Bloody Marys
I pour a Jamison for Claudia
A Scotch for myself
Adjust the lighting
And for the next hour
And more
We are in the room of our own making
Somewhere in the air
Between Rochester and St. Paul
Our own space with no interruptions
Toasts and laughter
Concerns and questions
We somehow crack
The barrier
Of glass, metal
And plastic

It is only on "goodbye"
We return to reality
Air hugs
No back pats
No cheeks to kiss

The Zen of Spaghetti Sauce

Dreary Sunday after virtual church
No walk today
The perfect time
For Perrella family red sauce—"sugo"
With our adaptations
Of course!

Start by roasting a rack of ribs
Rubbed with salt, pepper, herbs
Next, mix ground beef, bulk Italian Sausage
An egg, Judy's breadcrumbs
Mash and mix
Mash and mix
Mold into meatballs on a baking sheet
Ready to go when the ribs come out

Then chop, chop chop
Mince, mince, mince
Garlic, carrots, peppers
Sure you could use the Cuisinart
But speed is not the point
Details!
Slice onion into thin crescents
Puree Roma tomatoes

Get out the big Dutch oven
Not that one
The tall 8-quart one
Add oil
Saute garlic, onions
Carrots and peppers

Have you forgotten about
Coronavirus yet?
No? then you are not properly
Engaged
Focus!
Add pureed tomatoes

Add canned tomatoes
Tomato paste
Herbs
More herbs
A little red wine
Or in this case, the ever-ready
Sangria
Stir
Taste
More salt?
Pepper?
Simmer

In the meantime
Make phone calls
Have a virtual happy hour

Check sauce
Stir
Hang out some more

Add ribs and Meatballs
More phone calls
More stirring
Until rib meat falls off the bone

Sneak a meatball
Cook the pasta

Plate it up in shallow bowls
A rolling prairie hill
Of noodles
A rib or two on the side
Generous ladle of sauce
Meatballs at the summit
Parmesan the crowning touch

Place the bowl on TV tray
Napkins? Silverware?

Open a bottle of Italian red
Pour into jam-jar glasses
Sip to make sure it is OK

Twist and roll that first forkfull
Do you miss the press conferences
The nightly news?
Are you thinking about
Being shut in
Getting sick?
If yes
You are not in the zen space
Focus
Have another meatball

TP

Investing in these days?
Choose paper product futures
With a high percentage
On toilet paper
And Kleenex

No problem finding
Produce
Meat, fish
Eggs and dairy
Bubbly water aisle
Still has big bottles
And six packs

But turn the cart into the last aisle
And the land of plenty
Vanishes
Shelves skeletal
Missing their guts
Rolls and rolls
Of paper
Baggies
Even paper plates
All gone
All gone away

Signs admonish us
only one four pack per cart
Lucky us! A shelf surgeon
Fighting the endless battle
To keep shelf guts in place
Has just opened a case
No matter it is not
The cushy stuff
The bluebears on TV
Wax romantic about
It is pure and simple butt—wipe
What you might find

In porta potties
Or locker rooms
But who's to complain?
Just imagine
What this pack would bring
On the street front
Brown market?

Porch Concert

Warm and Sunny
A shame to stay indoors
Already taken our walk
So what?
Music stand
Loose-leaf binder
And "Chantal"
My cedar-top
Twelve-string guitar
And presto!
Instant neighbor concert
An audience of six
Seven if you count the cell phone
Video feed to St. Cloud

Here we are
Singing along
Chatting, laughing
Across the yards and porches
No one sulky
Or lonely
Or worried
Or afraid
Feeling shut in
It is what we all do best
In this time
Of staying in place
Finding ways to interact
Sharing joy
Being neighbors

Park Bench

It is our destination
Just a bit more than half-way
In our little daily walk
One of the few benches
On the lake side of the walkway
Children on bikes and scooters
Chatty clumps of teacher pals
Joggers huffing
All behind us instead
Of in our faces

Here we rest and reflect
Take it in
A pair of Mallards
Looking for a homestead
A small flock of Wood Ducks
Faces painted
Slicked-back hairdos
Parade along the shoreline

We plan for dinner
The night's entertainment
Avoid politics
The daily muck
Wonder about the kids
Promise to clean up the house
Just sit
In companionable silence
Taking in the lake
Sunlight
And the prayer shawl of assurance
We are not alone

Labyrinth

The Lake path is getting too crowded
A different route then
Under the Lexington bridge
And cross-country
Up the hill
To the dry pond
Veer to the right
Then left towards
The pedestrian bridge

Here a vantage point
Overlooking the Pavillion
The lake
Away from path traffic
In fact, all traffic
A place of respite
The Global Harmony Labyrinth

We walk the path tracing
Back on itself
It demands quiet
And focus
Thinking nothing at all
Except the fall of footsteps
The hairpin turns
Step by step
Weaving back and forth
A mental warp and weft

No wonder then
when we are done
we just sit
breathe
let the experience
soak deep
deep
before returning
to the spinning world
and traffic

Seventy-Nine Percent Reduction

Less than a week after
Shelter in place
The newspaper reports
In Minneapolis and St. Paul
Automobile traffic
Reduced seventy-nine percent
We feel it
Hear it

Even though we can't
See it
Like the satellite photos
Over China
The air smells sweeter
Late night trains
Early morning utility
Back-up beeper
No longer
Part of the hissing background
But center stage
And the mic turned up
It makes us wonder
If habits
Changed for now
Could stay in place
Inertia of the new reality
Once the order is lifted
And people can return
To life before
The shutdown?

Prep

It seems that all we have is time
But that would be a huge misconception
Scanning, uploading downloading
Saving files
All take extra time
And making videos
When everything is working
a download and upload
gets it where it needs to be

Of course
Everything does not work
All the time
In the first week
Schoology and Seesaw
Go down
And that's before all
The rest of us on Spring break
Comeback online

Like the rule of thumb for
Broadcast production
Each minute on the air
An hour of production time
Add in online meetings
Checking re-dos
Time for a mental health break
And a walk
It's a whole day's work and more
If you count the hours
Of lost sleep
It's
24-7 prep time

Masks

Brother Brian comes through
With an unlikely
But now needed gift
China's overproduction
Results in boxes of face masks
To our door

And now
It seems
Face masks
The new fashion
In areas of traffic

So a venture out
Wal-Mart
Prescriptions
A trial for our new gifts

Foggy glasses
Itchy chin
Uncertainty
Put then on in the car?
Just before we leave the car?
And what then?
Leave them on until we get home?
Questions
Questions

We do okay
I think
Re-set the calculation clock
For time of exposure
First symptoms
Putter about
Bags in quarantine
The front porch

Oh Shoot!

Risk takes on a new definition
Limiting time shopping
In proximity to others
Forgetting items
More than just exasperation
Another trip
Another mask used up
Another venture
Into potential exposure

Even with lists
and checking twice
consulting what we can get
in one place instead
of several
Limiting door handles
Even numbers
Of bags
Seems good
Preventative maintenance
We get home, and still it's
"Oh shoot!"

Of course
In these days
it's not just "Oh shoot"
that has altered understanding

The other word
With heightened
Meaning
Even more dubious
And dire in implication
"Seems"

Magnolia in Waiting

I had thought by now
With days of warm temperatures
The Magnnolia would burst out
A popcorn bush
White blossoms exploding out
Of the patient buds

But no
Not yet
Cautious
As if heeding the governor's
Edict
Too many of us blooms
In very close proximity

Still, I check
Each morning
Look for signs
A bud splitting
A white petal-let
A scent in the morning breeze
But no
Not yet

"Why?" I ask
"You are missing
Basking in these days
Of soft winds
Sun-filled sky
And for now
A distinct reduction
In automobile exhaust
Pollution—
What could possibly
Be your excuse?"

The answer comes
Not from buds

But from sky
Camouflaged
By greys of cloudy
Dusk,
Flurry of snow
Dusting the ground
And the wise,
Patient, Magnolia

Third Weekend

Something different today
Traffic is about the same
But step outside
Laughter, chatter
Children in the park
Different than the weekdays
Here's Jack on a hunt for rocks
Looking tres chic in shades
Two year-old girl
Runs off from her family
Already her own self
Family tries (in vain)
To get a kite aloft
A mom patiently walks the labyrinth
Focusing on the task at hand
And daughter
And dog
All the things of a weekend Saturday
In this time
Surreal

And So It Begins

Day one
D-Day for teachers
And I hit the wrong beach
Computer freezes
Videos don't go
All the things that worked
Last week
Crash and burn
More Dunkirk
than Normandy

Then, *coup de grace*
I lose all of my online classes
Revert to old school
Email
Slightly newer school
Google Docs
To conduct classes

And then like all battles
The rebuilding begins
Into the evening
Reconstructing classes
More emails
More logins
More more more
Snore

Payback

It's why we do it
Even through coronavirus
Computer crashes
Work and more work

The last day of the quarter
Google Meet
And oh
The children
Their faces
Energized voices
Stumbling over each other
Like the waters
At Goosebery Falls
Tumbling with ideas
And follow-ups
And flashes of neurons
Like photos at the Oscars

And all in an hour of contained
Chaos
You forget the detritus of a week
Where nothing seemed to work
And every corner presented
Another conundrum

This
This is payback
For not enough pay
And too many hours
With a waiting partner
Across town

This is something
The one percent
Will never know

This something
Up off our backs
Dusting ourselves off
And waking early

Fourth Weekend

It is the weekend
That is the reason
Our faith
Yearns for church, mosque, synagogue
Our Holy places
Especially in these times
We all feel
As if we have been entombed
In our own houses
Time to reflect
What is true
What is
Most important

Politicians balance commerce
Over human life
While we with houses
And food
And toilet paper
Must give pause
Consider
Those without even these
We take for granted
Time to roll away
The stone that separates
Us from the world
Time to grow up
Throw away childish things
And in this time
Of sheltering away from the world
Resurrect ourselves
Understand
The hard truth
Of Easter

Email

Ubiquitous and temporary
A bad excuse for face – to – face
Or a real letter
It is expedient
Convenient
And deletable

Then there comes
Every now and then
An email
You want to print and save

Like this one

Former student now in middle school
Out of the blue
Writes to ask
How I am doing
So unexpected
I re-read
Not a "hi, bye"
Not a "just checking in"
A reaching out
For connection
Though we try not to have favorites
We are human
And this one is
Special

Concerts

From the Mayo Clinic
To the local orchestras
Rockers
And folkies
Everyone spills out their music
Onto YouTube, Zoom
Google Meets
Facebook
Putting out more
Than just distraction
It is sharing hope
And giving joy

So Deni again
On Good Friday's evening
The darkest time
Of the Christian year
She plays
Dances
Sings
Invites us into her place
Her soul of music

Never mind the technical glitches
It is the communal joy
Seeing the comments scroll
On the sidebar
From places like Brazil, France, and Australia
All in this space
"Hey now, don't dream it's over…"
Deni sings
And we concur

Inspired, on Saturday
The music stand
On the porch
Claudia makes a drink
Hauls out the plastic chairs for

44

Would-be attendees
And songs go out
Into the neighborhood

Passerby, even the kid down the block
Not sure
What to make of it
But the neighbors get it
They clap and cheer
Not so much the high caliber
Of the singing
Or even the brash voice of the twelve-string
It is pumping the fist
At the disease
The joining of voices
Our inoculation

And at the end
We are
Warren Zevon's
Werewolves
Howling in unison at COVID
"This is our hood
Our territory
You best stay away
Far away
AH-OOOO!"

Nature Program

The God in charge of weather
Thinks we need variety
Delivers entertainment
The day after porch concert
We wake up to snow
Like confectioner's sugar
Dusting the park

Our kitchen window
Nature show
The micro-climate
Changing day by day
What's on today?
The usual cast of squirrels, chickadees,
Sparrows, finches

And the guest actors
Boss Robin back to claim his birdbath
The plodding muskrat
From under the deck
Teenage cardinals testing
Their independence from the nest
A hawk perhaps if we are lucky
Then hangers on from last season
Returning to our screen
The squadron of geese heading for the lake
Warblers we hope
And orioles, grackles
Bold rabbits, chipmunks
In time, the hummingbirds
The constant flowing cast
Of characters
Filling our giant screen
Keeping us in wonder
Fending off the deadly monotony
Of closed doors

Easter

Easter service arrives via laptop
We watch from the
Kitchen counter
Sipping coffee
In lieu of holy wine
Munch on croissants
The body of Christ

Sarah chooses the story
Mary at the tomb
Fearful the body
Has been stolen
Denied sacred rites
She weeps
Tear-filled eyes
Seeing, she thinks the gardener
Instead of the miracle

Like Mary we search
But we do not see
The miracle is here and now
Not some two millennia
In the past
It is the budding magnolia
Holding out against the
Late spring snow
It is Boss Robin
At the birdbath
The wood ducks'
Tiny fleet paddling the lake fringe

It is now
In Sarah's joyful
Emphatic voice
"Go forth!
Do your job!"

Ordinary Time

After Easter the church says
It is now "ordinary time"
Ordinary by what?

Will we ever
Go back to ordinary
As it was before the virus
Or are closed doors
Social distancing
The new ordinary
In this extraordinary time?

Will we ever shake hands
Embrace
Pat each other on the back
Gather together?

When will hot dogs and a beer
At a baseball game
Be ordinary?
Or weddings
Graduation
Easter dinner
Fireworks

Questions unanswered
Just vague projections
Of the peak
And then what?
The gradual slope
Yes but safe?

When will it be safe
For ordinary measures
Safe for our
Ordinary lives?

Monday Again

Another Monday
Black coffee
Click the keyboard
Lo and behold! Things work
Classes almost in place
The lag much less than the last
cutting and pasting
Downloading and uploading
Even the video works

It is almost enough
To sit back
Almost enough
To let the breath out
Only minor glitches
Students respond almost
Instantaneously

The key word
Almost
In the back of the head
Rat brain lurks
Clawing
"Don't be so sure,"
It wheedles
"Don't relax,"
It whispers
"It's only Monday after all"

Coyotes on Michigan Ave.

Chicago's main drag of commerce
Looks like downtown St. Paul
On a Sunday evening
Not a car in sight
No pedestrians either
The semaphores click green, amber. red
For no purpose whatsoever

And here's a coyote
Ambling along
Right down the middle
of the Michigan Avenue
Why not?
Who's gonna stop it?
Ol' Wylie
Not chasing Roadrunner
Taking his time
Window shopping
Coat's getting a little ragged
Maybe some flashier shoes ?
Slim pickin's for dinner though
Restaurants closed
Not so much tossed, dropped
Thrown out in back of fancy digs
Gotta settle for fast food
Fight off them damn seagulls
Maybe head for the west side
try different cuisine
Fewer gulls there anyway

Leavening

After Easter, we all want to rise
But Duluth is out of yeast
We go back to the days of unleavened bread
tortillas and pita
flour made from left over
tailings from brewing
curious, creative beings

Virtual Poetry Reading

Of course, because I am the host
The computer will not work
Cursing and sweating
Thank god it's the mic
Leaving me mute
And fuming
I scribble a sign
Hold it up to the camera
"Getting another computer
Go ahead"

And so they do

While I find a back door way
To load Zoom
Set it up, login
Only ten minutes late
To my reading
I cover with a welcome
The first reader
Like a story tease
before the opening credits
except
this isn't NCIS
It is real people
With real words
No hitches on their part

In split screen I see
All their faces how they react
To each other's verse
How the grasp the subtle humor
With a nod
A smile
And then, it is not so bad
Not a disaster

A learning yes

On so many levels
Which computer to avoid
Mid program ad-libbing
Appreciating
What is there
Voices
Faces
Words with meaning
The joy of celebrating
In this month of poetry
Virtual in place
But not in spirit

Madame Lachrymosa

Her expression doesn't change
Leaning against the fence
Propped up by brick and stone
Misery is nothing new to her
Cold and left out
Unsheltered
She shares a prayer
For all those
On the streets
Sleeping in hammocks
Tents and soggy boxes

Prays
Her rosary
Offering an *Ave Maria*
For the suffering newcomers
And for once is glad
She is not flesh and bone
Does not have to wake
In early morning hours
Wondering about food
And shelter and the next paycheck
She does not need a mask
Virus on her surface will not penetrate
Her stony surface

And yet
There she stands
Her desolate pose
Admonishing
Our worries petty
In the face of others
Life and death
We are among the lucky
The stone lady
By the fence a reminder
The poor
You shall always have
Among you

Fifth Weekend

Yellow dots the Forsythia
Fingerlets of white
On the Magnolia
After a wintry week
Spring grabs another toe-hold
In the climbing wall
Of Minnesota seasons

An icy slip of four days
Resolved by sunshine
The southwest wind
April continues its climb
Magicking away the stubborn
Patches of hiding snow

Climbing and pulling
With it trailers of green
Bringing smiles to the gardener

The tulips
And irises have survived
Deep-rooted prairie grass
Stretches out of softening earth
A sun salute to the season

Grown Up Books

After nearly a month
Of bedtime reading
I have run out of children's books
What now?
I am out of practice
With adult level tomes
The typeface denser
More ink to the page
The book certainly feels
Weightier

Crack the binding
Flip through first pages
And then plunge in
It is bracing
Diving into a forgotten lake
Finding the currents familiar
Perhaps more water
Before toe touches
Sandy bottom
Perhaps even over the head

No matter
The mind and body adjust
Rising to the surface
Perhaps more strenuous
Strokes to keep afloat
But float I do
Deeper into the book

Routine

So the days melt into routine
Me, up around seven
Shower if needed and a shave
On sleepy days, a small pot
Of strong, black coffee

Next hit the computer
2nd and 3rd grades first
Because they are easier
To do—a way to wakeup
Into the teaching day
Video, sure
Then 4th and 5th grade math
Finish with reading

Now Claudia is awake
One of us makes coffee
English muffins
Scones or crumpets
Butter
Maybe peanut butter
Jam
Morning meds

Some days defined
By video meetings
Classes or teacher-mates
A quick munch
Start correcting
Feedback

Think about dinner
What do we need?
Break to venture out
Cub?
Trader Joes?
Liquor store?
Hardware store?

A walk to the labyrinth perhaps
Late afternoon tea
Putter
Keep correcting
My God! How has the day
Run away with the hours
So plentiful when sipping coffee?
Putter
A nap maybe
Think dinner
Prep
Cook
Make TV trays
Eat
Watch
Do dishes
Massage for Claudia
Stretches for me
Evening ablutions
Read
Lights out
Repeat

Until the weekend knocks
Surprising us
Out of the routine

Glimmers

Hope abides
A mother comes through the virus
Still unable to smell or taste
But past the fever and pain
Jokes about the grossness of food in mouth
But no flavor
No aroma
Humor still the best tonic
While she looks to her front line
Job
Not in the hospital
But on the streets delivering the mail

And across town
A baby
Can't wait for the appointment
Jumps into this world
Bringing life in the time of death
And joy
In the time of despair

Small signs perhaps
In the great scheme of things
But vital
Any uplift in the psyche
Another face mask
A shield
A shift in the soul
Against the dis-ease

Earth Day 2020

How shall we celebrate
Earth Day
In this time of turning away
Closing out
Sheltering in place?

Look! Take in
The example before us
With humans more and more
Out of the picture
The air is sweeter
The water clearer
Animals reclaim their territory

What if
What if
When the all clear sounds
We try
Really try
To replicate the world as it is
Now
Making our presence
As invisible as possible?

Adley

In this time of staying in
Staying put
A new life won't have any of it
Coming before her time
Adley
"God is just"
Bursts into the world
Life is justice
Life is meaning
Life is choices

And what choice
Do we make
To insure
That
Adley, the justice of God
Prevails?

Spring Comes Regardless

Spring doesn't care about microorganism
Doesn't matter that we are shut in
In fact, it enjoys the cleaner air
The smaller percentages
Of toxins in the runoff
The lack of clamor
Quiet
The spring likes quiet
Pushes out magnolia blooms
forsythia
Dandelions in the park
Regreening the world

It's Official...

...no back to school this year
No graduation ceremonies
No retirement celebrations
No tunnel of teachers' arms
Waving the students out the bus line

These rites of passage
In silence and mostly alone
Define this generation
Everything's different

My own year-end rituals
Abandoned
No pizza parties
No chess tournament in Math
No last day circle of fith graders
Instead, a meeting online

The ceremony of the memory rocks
Not hand to hand
But left on doorsteps

It is contrary
To the calling
It's supposed to be face to face
Teacher and students
Everyone learning
In the safety zone
Of the classroom

Now safety is not school
Teaching turned inside out
And yet
Here we are
Everyday

Teacher and students
Reaching
Reaching
Virtual hands grasping
For each other
For learning yes
But more and more
For comfort

A New Bench

Our new rest stop
Away from the lake path
And crowds of strollers, joggers
Bikes and skaters
Positioned just so
Downside of a hill
Sheltered by evergreen boughs
A strategic respite
Far away enough from the labyrinth
To respect the
Zen moment
Of anyone walking the winding path
Close enough to be next in line

There is evidence
Of other's pause here
A hair scruffy
Wrappers empty water bottles
But it is always vacant
Upon our arrival
Waiting to hold us in rest
Until we are ready
To walk the labyrinth's
Path refreshed and prepared

Labyrinth in the Rain

OK it's not a serious rain
Barely a sprinkle
The air neither fresh nor muddy
Smells gray
The slightly ozone scent
Falling as we turn in and again
Steps focusing senses

Here, a call robin to robin
Sparrow chatter
The wingbeat of Canadian geese
Car wheel swish
chat of passersby
fade into the turning
inward, inward and then the release
of the outward swoop
connecting the yin and yang
earth and water
our feet
and our souls
the in and out
of the labyrinth

Sixth Weekend

Can it be?
Six weekends mark the time
A quarter of a school year
Nearly spent

Sad students don't
Join the online meeting
And those that do
Don't have much to say

So what to do?
A pomegranate martini
Friday evening
With Deni's violin
The backdrop
Is a temporary tonic
Arkansas-style burgers
Chips and a beer

Sustenance
Enough to go on
But not celebratory
Getting by
But not thriving
Day to day
But not planning of te future

Planning
Thriving
Celebrating
All need proximity
Shared time
Shared touch
Things we hunger for
now out of reach

Skate Boys

We have seen them a couple of times
Three teen-age boys
Two inline skaters, one hockey puck
The tallest moves like Nathan Chen
The first time we saw him
Gliding around the labyrinth
We sat and watched
Not wanting to interrupt
Only when he came to the bench
To ruffle Rocky, the Dobermann
Did we dare approach

The boys are polite
Obsequious even
With gentle apologies
They move off
To a respectful distance
Huddle around their blue
Toyota Corolla
Grab some snacks
Head up the path

After our meditations
Coming off the labyrinth
They are on the next hillock
Pleasantries and thanks exchanged
We walked home
Confessed our prejudice
Against young men in slouching pants
Hanging in the park
Chastised, we are glad when
On another sunny afternoon
We spot the blue car
And encounter them
On the same turf
With joy instead of trepidation

Project

Claudia it seems needs a project
Sister obliges with a jar
Of sourdough starter
We had no idea
What we were in for

"Give it a name," said sister
So Womph it became
And Womph it is
Flour, water, yeast
And lactobacilli
Fed and watered,
Left overnight
Like the virus, it doubles by morning

"Throw away the top half"
Sister insttucts,
"and then you must feed it some more."
Frustrated
Nowhere near bread
A plan for crackers emerges

Womph is not in a hurry
Will not be rushed into work
Especially if just fed
Bubble, bubble
Time and more time
Even when dough is made
Womph reposes for hours
Worrying Claudia
That he is too wet
Not at all like the nicely
Polite doughball on YouTube

And so we wait
In suspense
What will Womph have wrought
When he gets fired up
And forms a golden crust?

Cast of Characters

We are among the regulars
At the labyrinth
The skater boys
Keep respectful distance
But visible
As is their blue Ford Focus
Mistaken earlier for a Toyota
They come with or without
Rocky the Doberman
Recognize us with a wave
Or stop for a chat

Across the way weary gramps
Worms his way into his book
Trying to shut out
Screeching grandkids
Careening on scooters or bikes
You can hear them across
The hillock back towards
The stone bridge

Now here's the solitary walker
Taking the winding pathway
Seriously
Reverential
Absorbed in midful meditation
Namaste

All this making a little
Strange community
With the weaving path
At its center
Diverging purposes
But sharing
A tie of recognition
A bond of place

News Item

Doctor on the front lines
Saving lives, takes her own
Why?
The answer is speculation
But I think on target.
She has worked for week and weeks
no end in sight
But sees hope if all people stay home
Flatten the curve

Then the president pops his mouth
Magical thinking masked as truth
His legions take to the streets
Governors open beaches, businesses
When they have no evidence
Lacking science
As well as human compassion

So this doctor
This hero
Seeing the tide turn against her
Against her calling
In anguish
Imagines
Hundreds and thousands
More put at risk
Thousands of body bags
Stacked in makeshift mortuaries
No exit
Except the door she chooses

Why why why?
And why isn't the president
And why aren't his lackeys
And why aren't the cowering governors
Charged
As accessories to suicide
Of more accurately
Co-conspirators to murder?

Distance Learning Reveals the Hidden Boy

Well a discovery in all of this
Teaching via keyboard
and thirteen-inch screen
Second grader
Removed from the distraction
Of his audience of peers
Beneath all the limbs akimbo silliness
Here is a scholar
Thinking deep into the well
Pulling imaginative images
From his magician's baseball cap
And getting it down
In print and illustration

Concrete proof
That teachers need to work beyond
What we see in the classroom
Need to find that space
For our students where they show
The shine of their gifts
The sparkle of their talents

Queues

Social distancing has become habit
Even in Costco
A one-way lineup
Of grocery carts files
Along the meat cooler
Starting at the beef end working through
Lamb and then pork
Ending at bratwurst and deli items
The pace deliberate
Not helter-skelter like normal times
Check-out lines marked off
Tape every six feet

Morelli's too
Backed up deli counter
No grumbling
In fact, it seems
Coronavirus
Has taken tight-lipped Minnesota
And moved it to Chicago
Strangers with something else
To talk about than the weather
Engage in conversation:
"You like that horseradish cheese, huh?"
"What beer ya got there?"
"How about them gallon bags of spaghetti sauce?"

Giving room, slower pace
Having a chat
A different sense of time
And space
A more civilized
New reality
Perhaps?

Happy Hour at a Social Distance

Well it is nearly six feet
And we are four people
Who are careful
And it has been over a month
Since face to face

So here we sit on the front porch
Cocktails
Hors d'oeuvres
And a sunny afternoon
Discussing matters of weight
Politics
My job
Family
Sourdough

The talk is really secondary
To the laughter
The small gesture
That would be lost on the
Thirteen-inch screen
The camaraderie
On the porch
Together
While the world
Whirrs on down Lexington

Distance Learning Opens Some Doors

Like my second grader last week
Doors opening
like the tulips in the front garden
cupping sunlight

The shy girl
not being drowned out
by gregarious classmates
Startles with a sure voicing
clear and confident
So filled with emotion
I catch my breath
Before I replay the recording
And again, so Claudia
Can appreciate
The art of the delivery

The always needs help
Math student
Creates a masterful map
A cartographer would applaud
Streets and neighborhood
With flair and precision

Where does this come from?
I wonder
But I already know the answer:
From the blank canvas
The empty spaces
And no one else
Competing to fill it up
Making way
For the hidden genius
Of the child in the corner

Scents and Sense-ability

Last week the labyrinth smelled
Like the brown of recent rainfall
Sodden earth
Another day
Then it smelled like the gray
Of droplets on pavement
Yesterday smelled like
Linens washed in the lake
And hung to dry
Just steps away from the cabin

Today the labyrinth smells of birdsong
Trilling lark, warbler?
Chipping sparrow
Gossiping robins
And cardinals
An elusive scent
On the breeze
Flavored with afternoon sunlight
The olfactory organs
Work to identify
A word more precise
But birdsong will have to do
As I refocus on the steps
And the turnings
Moving inwards and back towards release

Seventh Weekend

Gradually the world becomes green
Last week, a lone dandelion in the park
And now a galaxy of miniature suns
Glow in their greening firmament
Accented by patches of Creeping Charlie
And Canadian Violet

And in the garden, early bloomers
Sing their songs of color—
Golden tulips
Magenta fritillary
Uncurling violin headstock
Of fern
And pointy tongues of hosta

How can the gardener
Be sullen in this springing forth?
A daily inspection
Watching for new sproutings
Repairing gangly trellises
Even picking up the jetsam
from traffic on Lexington
Part of the happy song he hums
"Dum, dum, diddly dee, dum, dum"
Lost in the sunny place
the virus cannot breach

Communion

First Sunday
Communion Sunday
During virtual church
The minister uses banana bread
and water from a stainless steel bottle

We for once, one up the church
Homemade sourdough bread
freshly sliced
and sangria
our holy wine

Golf

Golfers are ecstatic
The links open
In the gradual phase-in
Of re-opening

I wish I could share their joy
Now that the door
Has cracked back open
How much more pressure
to open more
and more doors
How many people
Taking more risks
Or as one doctor puts it
How many
What number
Is the number of acceptable deaths?

Traffic

More cars
More people moving about
How many on urgent business?
How many flaunting
Stay at home?
We fall in between
Could we get along
Without a trip to Osceola?
Sure
Is it good for us?
Yes
And good for a small business?
Is it urgent?

Hairs to split
In this unknown time
Definitions redefined
what is need
What is necessary
Goods for the body
Good for the soul
What is more important?

And what if a trip
Over roads and highways
Achieves everything?

A Visit

Michael arrives
Of course, it's dinnertime
And a debate begins
Who has he seen?
Where has he been?
We do sort-of
Social distancing
As he presents cards
A print
Other items to share
And I bite the bullet
Offer dinner
Just made curry chicken
More chats
We ease up just a bit
Angry with ourselves
So cautious with family
Offspring, for heaven's sake!
And angry with the virus
With slow moving officials
That it should come to this
And then
Food for the road
In a paper bag,
He is off
Leaving us worried
Relieved
But no less angry

Reading Material

We ponder
Searching for the just right
Words
Just the right touchpoints
Of thought and emotion
To use for
These students
In this time

Books that address their needs
Avatars for us
In the home classroom

We cannot embrace them all
Let alone
The one who has retreated
Checked out
Google meets and one to one
Texting
Means comforting now

An air hug
Over distance
Through walls
Of boredom, fear and despair
The spark they will recognize
As us
Their teachers

May Vortex

A vortex in May
Usually means an early tornado
Down Hutchinson
Litchfield
Ripping up prairie sod

This year it's the polar type
over New England
blowing a wintry mix as far south
as the Georgia coast

Blowing March back in
Through the cracks in the window sill
Oh, if only we could go back
With what we now know
Back before ghost-town classrooms
When students
Filled the air
And the space
And we could give them all the things
We cannot give them anymore

The rites of passage
High school seniors on parade
Through the hallways and clusters
Certificates of recognition
Pizza parties
School picnic
The last day tunnel of cheers

Teacher Appreciation

No posters on the workroom door
No mystery treats in the mailbox
No peanut butter balls on the counter
Appreciation takes on a different form
Lawn signs
Drive by shout outs
Sure
But the real appreciation
More deep and subtle
A new thinking in parents' minds
An understanding of
What goes into our days
And evenings and weekends
Why we are so tenacious
About growth and learning
Why the hours
And energy
And hard-earned dollars spent
For too much time
And not enough recompense
Why we do not call it
A job

Marchaprilmay

Today is all of spring quarter
The greening of May
The optimistic sun of April
The bluster of March
Even from the labyrinth
Lake Como tires to emulate
The big lakes
Steely blue and moody
The northern scent of pine
More predominant
And cardinals' calls
Fill the park

A perfect day
As metaphor
Time out of joint
Seasons swirl
of their own accord
Black bears sniff out
Locked down malls
Shoots green the garden
As flocks of leaves
Fly by like scared sparrows
A chill
Even as the sunlight warms
The walkers home

Dandelion Metaphors?

I muse as we walk
Recalling a single dandelion
A few days ago
And now the park grounds
Lit up by hundreds
Upon hundreds
Of tiny suns
Wouldn't they make
An interesting parallel
A metaphor even
For COVID?

"Absolutely not!"
A surprisingly fierce reaction
From Claudia
"Yes, they are weeds
To you gardeners
But what harbingers
Of hope they are!
Do not compare them
to death and disease!"

Of course, she is right
The constellations in the fields
A beacon signaling
To dormant buds
And sprouts
That all is well
Safe now to burst forth

Like Mercury
The herald
Delivering good news
The world yet lives
Plant, animal
And yes
Even us the virus carriers

Eighth Weekend

We wake early
Even though it is cold and grey
Snow in New England
Frosty even in Alabama
Our goal—Trader Joe's before ten
The one time creaking bones and sore hips
Have advantage these days
Over sleeker shoppers—
We have first dibs to the store

We drop the hyper-vigilance
Six feet please
Six feet please
We roll down aisles
Unencumbered
No need to wait for greens
Or bubbly water
Steering around shelf-stockers
Shopping done
Before the masses come

Mother's Day

Pearl makes herself known
One of the last
In the shop
No time to look carefully
Before the flowers are wrapped
Gingerly handed over

So a surprise at the mausoleum
Unwrapped
The flowers embrace a plastic Dragonfly

We know this is not coincidence
Pearl came to us in this form
In the parking lot
Pearl Park by Diamond Lake
After dad's memorial
Flitting in and out
A cursive code
Repeated here
"We are fine
And we are safe"

It is the comfort we seek
The parents rest untouched by contagion
Their presence palpable
Their blessings:
Calm, quiet,
And peace

So peace back to Pearl and Jim
And to Margaret, Marguerite, and Jean
Phyliss, Sumi, and Michi

All that you are
Still lives in your learning
Still walks in your wake
Still thrives in your thinking
Still learns from your living
Peace to you all
Who bring us peace
Who gave us life

Insomnia

The teacher tosses
Sheds blankets
Wraps them back close
Anxieties--kids not in class
Lessons undone
A year in limbo
As is the year to come
What if
What if
What if?
Amygdala in high gear
Woody Allen brain
"Where does the universe expand?"
Sicilian sausage pizza doesn't help
When the brain isn't over thinking
Stomach is grumpy
Gurgling and growling

Do I take any comfort
My colleagues commiserate
In their own beds?
Worrying who we missed
What we didn't think of
What we over-thought
How to do it all
How to do anything
Rollover
2:30
Rollover
3:17

Various interventions tried
Most don't work
We know the only real cure
Back in our zone
Of the classroom
And all those chatty
Quizzical, amazing young people
Looking up
For what will be revealed

Missing

The skate boys haven't been
Here all week
Not that we worry
They are skating
Most likely in the park
Somewhere, just not here

It is a missing element though
The grand scheme of trees
and water
breezes more southerly
sparrow chirps and grackle cackle
the human interaction
just enough
It is good to see you
Content in your gliding arcs
And boyish charm

Water Feature

A new sound as we walk the labyrinth
New bird
Trilling—a cardinal?
But not the same
We track it to a budding tree
On the hill's downward slope
Spooked, it flits across our
Measured path
Mental note:
Sparrow sized but slimmer
Fork in the tail
Our only clue
Remember to check
The Sibley Guide at home

More sounds
Water now flows
The concrete lagoon
Giving purpose
To the arching bridge
A backdrop for our
Contemplative steps
Unnatural, but fitting somehow
Into this landscape
And soundscape

Flowing water
Bird call
Wind rustle
Our footsteps

All there
An open stage set
And we the players
Between acts
Sit on the bench
Enjoy the show

Necessary Goods

So it seems coffee is a necessary
Commodity, and that the shop
In Linden Hills
Is a necessary service

A sense of relief
The coffee snob rejoices
No stooping
Grocery store beans
No drab
In our cups

But it is more than that
Over forty years
Of commiseration
Coffee, tea of course
But also, offspring
Boys weaving wayward
Comings and goings
Growing up
Both man and business
Folding back to the
Beginning
The source
Just a man and a dream

Ninth Weekend

Foreboding and joy
A full academic quarter in place
Foreboding at what
The governor's soft opening
Happens next week
What then?
Will people still take precautions?
Stay at home
Keep separate
In groups
Smaller than ten?

Or will it be like recess after
Weeks and weeks of rain
Everyone kids on the playground
Let loose
The devil, too, romping
Along side
Raising his glass with glee

And yet--
Baltimore orioles
Chortle from tree to tree
On the labyrinth's border
Cabbage white butterfly
In the greening garden
Geraniums in the front stoop pots
Boxes of annuals on the back porch
Awaiting resettlement
Neighbors singing along
Requesting encores
Relishing the company
Of voices in song

May 18

Two months in
The Governor says it's time
A gradual opening
A good place to stop
(Though the virus does not stop)
And so we watch
Another spike
In the making
People pushing through
Walmart doors
No six feet here
And only a few masks

A good place to stop
(Though the virus does not stop)
Churches in defiance
Not for saving souls
Or communion
But for filling the pews
Reviving the collections
Never mind the congregation's peril
A thousand micro droplets
For every chink of silver
The devil shares the chalice
with priest and communicants

A good place to stop
(Though the virus does not stop)
It takes advantage of
Clandestine graduation celebrations
Packed Packer bars
Protests on the Capitol steps
Twenty somethings who think
They're immune
Shoppers leaning in
At the farmers market

A good place to stop
(Though the virus does not stop)
No bulls careening down streets in Pamplona
No take me out to the ballgame
No foot-long hotdogs, tom thumb donuts
No buckets of cookies or fries
No Space Needle or Giant Slide

A good place to stop
(Though the virus doesn't stop)
The virus doesn't give a shit
About official pronouncements
Political wrangling
The wheeze of the dying
It only knows self-perpetuation
Phase one is done
The virus goes on
A good place to stop

ACKNOWLEDGEMENTS

These poems are seeing their lives in hard copy for the first time, however the poem, "Shelter in Place" appeared online in Sagirah Shahid's artist/writer Facebook page, The Sunflower Room. Several poems have been read in online virtual readings, my Bridges series, co-hosted by Next Chapter Booksellers, the Bird's Nest Open Mic series, and The Basement Bar, hosted by Susan Cossette Eng. Sarah Campbell, Lead Minister at Mayflower UCC, has included several of these poems in her daily emails to the congregation.

The challenging sermons by Reverend Campbell and her Associate Minister, Christian Briones have served as seeds for several poems. Further inspiration comes from the virtual music concerts by New York violinist (and Mountain Stage Pal) Deni Bonet, and neighbors, Brianna and Kurt Jorgenson.

Thank you to all independent bookstores keeping it going through this time of isolation, but especially my home base, Next Chapter Booksellers. My other haunts include Subtext, Eat My Words, The Irreverent Bookworm, Birchbark Books, Moon Palace, Wild Rumpus, Red Balloon, and in Duluth, Zenith.

As I tell my students, editing is a huge part of any writing project. That task has been shared by my wife, Claudia Daly; poet/teacher pal. Mary Jo Thompson (who took it upon herself to edit the entire manuscript, when all I asked was to give it a look); and Liz at North Star Press. A gargantuan "thank you " to all!

Thanks Especially to the teachers, staff and students (and former students!) at Red Oak Elementary school in Shakopee, MN—this book is really for you!

As always, big thanks to my wife Claudia for late nights and early mornings when the muse hits, and for being editor par excellence!

STANLEY KUSUNOKI is the author of three collections of poetry: *Shelter in Place, Poems in a Time of COVID-19; Items in the News; and 180 Days, Reflections and Observations of a Teacher.* He has taught creative writing to young people through programs at The Loft, Asian-American Renaissance, Intermedia Arts, S.A.S.E., and The Write Place. He was a recipient of a Loft Asian-American Inroads mentorship and was awarded a Minnesota State Arts Board Cultural Collaboration grant to create, write, and perform *Beringia, the Land Bridge Project* with Ojibwe performance poet, Jamison Mahto, at Intermedia Arts. He is the host/curator of the Bridges Reading Series at Next Chapter Booksellers in St. Paul. Most recently, Kusunoki was the High Potential Coordinator at Red Oak Elementary School in Shakopee, Minnesota. He lives in St. Paul with his wife, Claudia Daly.